TWO COYOTES

TWO COYOTES

by Carol Carrick · illustrated by Donald Carrick

CLARION BOOKS
TICKNOR & FIELDS: A HOUGHTON MIFFLIN COMPANY
NEW YORK

ACKNOWLEDGMENTS:
Special thanks to Beth Parks, wildlife biologist, and to
Gus Ben David, director of the Felix Neck Wildlife
Sanctuary, for sharing their knowledge of New England
wildlife.

Clarion Books
Ticknor & Fields, a Houghton Mifflin Company
Text copyright © 1982 by Carol Carrick
Illustrations copyright © 1982 by Donald Carrick

Printed in the United States of America

Library of Congress Cataloging in Publication Data

Carrick, Carol.   Two coyotes.
Summary: Living along the edge of the forest, a male and
female coyote are forced into a desperate search for food
as they struggle to survive the bitterly cold eastern winter.
1. Coyotes—Juvenile literature. [1. Coyotes] I. Carrick,
Donald, ill. II. Title.
QL737.C22C37   599.74'442   81-38490
ISBN 0-89919-078-2   AACR2

For David and Lois Budbill

THE rim of the sky was tinted pink and gold by the setting sun. Along the edge of an eastern forest, a tired coyote trotted behind her mate.

It had been a hungry winter for the coyotes. During the rest of the year they could easily catch mice, insects, and

other small creatures to eat. In winter these were scarce, so the coyotes depended upon dead animals for much of their food.

But this year the winter had been mild. Few animals had died from illness or starvation.

A flock of crows in the clearing cast long shadows on the snow. As the coyotes approached, the crows rose with a clap of wings and settled in the bare branches of the trees.

Then the crow alarm sounded.

"CAW! C-A-A-W!"

At the sound, the male coyote stopped and sniffed the wind. His senses were sharp enough to smell a human hunter as far as a mile away. But the target of this noisy, flapping, dive-bombing squadron of crows was a great horned owl. The crows tormented the huge bird until he gave up his perch and disappeared into the forest.

The male coyote continued his search for food. He followed a pathway that a small herd of deer had trampled through the brush.

The female coyote flopped on the ground to rest. In a month and a half her first litter of pups would be born. If she did not get enough to eat, the pups growing inside of her might not survive.

As night closed in, the flock of crows slipped one by one into the forest. Soon the murmur of their voices and the rustle of their wings grew hushed. After their black shapes had melted into the darkness, the female coyote rose and stretched her stiff body.

Her parents had taught her how to hunt and she had learned the secrets of her territory. She knew where to locate the burrows of small animals, and where their trails led.

With her long, pointed nose to the ground, the coyote began
to follow a hare's runway.

Suddenly the hare exploded from his resting place beside a
rock. The startled coyote quickly recovered from her surprise
and gave chase.

The hare was faster. His bouncy gait could have kept him a safe distance from the coyote. But he panicked and started running in a circle. The coyote saved the last of her energy by following in a smaller circle. She saw the hare begin to tire. Then she pushed herself. With a burst of speed, she cut him off and knocked him down with her nose.

Just as her jaws were about to close on his throat, the hare made a last, frantic effort to get to his feet. He succeeded and was off. But the coyote was desperate, too, and she kept close behind.

Before the coyote could knock him to the ground again, the hare leaped. He changed direction in midair, then bounded to

the edge of the clearing, and slipped under a clump of raspberry bushes.

As fast as she was, the coyote was not an acrobat like the hare. It took her some time to find her way through the brambles. Then she picked up the hare's scent and followed his fresh tracks through the snow. But suddenly the tracks ended.

The bewildered coyote nosed around the tracks. What had happened to the hare? After he escaped from her, he had quietly loped off through the forest. And just as quietly, the great horned owl had struck from above. He hooked the hare with his talons and carried him away to his nest.

The hungry coyote had been cheated of her meal. Trembling with fatigue, she curled her tail around herself and lay down to sleep under a fallen tree. If she did not find food soon, she would become too weak to hunt. Before long she would starve.

Meanwhile, the male coyote had followed the trail through the brush to a cedar thicket where several families of deer were gathered. A doe was pawing at the ground, trying to reach a patch of grass.

Suddenly the alert coyote saw something. A field mouse had been nibbling roots under the snow, safe from the coyote's

searching eyes. But the doe had uncovered the mouse and blocked the snow tunnel to his burrow.

Now the mouse scrambled out onto the snow to avoid the digging hoofs. His dark form was easy to follow across the bright snow. In a second the pouncing paws of the coyote covered him. The mouse's squeak was swallowed in a gulp.

One mouthful was not enough to feed a hungry coyote. An anxious doe eyed him as her unborn fawn stirred inside her. The doe snorted, standing her ground, and the coyote backed off. He could not risk being slashed by the doe's sharp

hoofs. If he were injured, he might not be able to hunt.

Except for a second mouse, the hungry coyote caught nothing more that night. As the sun rose the next morning, he curled up in a sheltered spot. Warmed by the sun, he slept.

Across the valley, another animal lay on the snow. A group of deer had moved on during the night to a place where the trees had not been stripped of twigs and bark—the deer's winter food. But one old buck could not keep up. Even though the winter weather was mild, he had become sick and weak. He collapsed in the snow and the others moved on without him.

At noon a crow sailed over the valley. With the trees and bushes bared of leaves, it didn't take long before the crow spotted the dead buck. He made a few passes over the half-frozen carcass.

"CAW! CAW!"

Then he flew off to spread the news to the rest of the flock.

"CAW!"

Later, three crows flew over the male coyote's head. He followed them with his gaze. His ears pricked.

"CAW! CAW! CAW!"

On the other side of the valley a flock of crows called and
circled. Had they found food? The coyote licked his chops.

He crossed the deep snow in the valley gingerly, testing each drift with a paw to see if it would hold his weight. If he broke through the crust, his struggles would only sink him deeper into the snow until his remaining strength was used up.

When the coyote arrived on the other side of the valley, he found the crows pecking open the dead buck with their beaks. The coyote tried to drive them off, rushing at them and snapping his teeth. But the crows flapped easily out of his reach. And just as quickly, they settled back again.

In spite of the crows, the coyote had almost eaten his fill when another coyote appeared. The first coyote wagged his tail hopefully. Had his mate seen the circling crows? But then a low growl rumbled in his throat and the fur of his ruff bristled. It was not his mate, but a strange male that had been drawn to the spot.

The growl erupted as the first coyote sprang to his feet and rushed at the newcomer. The second coyote stopped. Slowly he lowered his hindquarters, hunched his back, and tucked his tail between his legs. Then the cowering animal crept forward. He flattened his ears and his eyes avoided the eyes of the other coyote.

The first coyote charged and the newcomer dropped to the ground. He rolled on his back, exposing his belly and throat. He didn't want to fight. The first coyote stood over him. His muzzle wrinkled and the corners of his mouth pulled back to bare his teeth in a horrible grin.

After a few last snarls, the first coyote trotted over to the buck and ate some more of the meat. This was to make clear that the food was his.

The loser withdrew to a respectful distance and lay down, hoping he would be allowed a turn at the tattered carcass.

The ears of both coyotes pricked when they heard a gentle wavering call. "Woo, woo, ooOOooo."

The first coyote recognized the voice of his mate. She was moving slowly across the snow. The male trotted toward her, wagging his tail in welcome. The female was too weary to give him her usual friendly greeting. She could only lick his face.

While the first coyote was distracted by the arrival of his mate, the other male slunk toward the carcass. The first coyote caught him trying to steal a scrap of meat. He attacked with such ferocity that the second coyote ran away for good.

The female ate eagerly while her mate stood guard. When she finished, she rubbed her muzzle clean on the snow. Then

the contented pair lay down side by side. The crows had saved them from another day of hunger.

Just after dark the coyote and his mate heard the first bark. "Yip, yip, oooOOOOOO."

Like an echo, a mournful howl answered from another direction, and then another, and another.

With a few barks, the male coyote added his voice to the chorus. Soon his mate joined him with her high-pitched wail.

Maybe they were sharing something with the other coyotes. Or maybe they sang for the sheer joy of it. We have no way of knowing. But winter was almost over and the two coyotes had survived. Soon their pups would be born and would thrive in the sunlight of their first spring.